The Letters of John and Jude

This is a self-study course designed to help you discover for yourself, from the Bible, some important basic truths concerning the books of I, II, III John and Jude.

how to study the lesson

1. Try to find a quiet spot free from distractions and noise.

2. Read each question carefully.

3. Look up the Scripture reference given after each question. Make sure you have found the correct Scripture passage. For example, sometimes you will find yourself looking up JOHN 1:1 instead of I JOHN 1:1.

4. Answer the question from the appropriate Bible passage. Write, in your own words, a phrase or sentence to answer the question. In questions that can be answered with a "yes" or "no" always give the reason for your answer . . . "Yes, because . . ."

5. If possible, keep a dictionary handy in order to look up words you don't understand.

6. Pray for God's help. You need God's help in order to understand what you study in the Bible. PSALM 119:18 would be an appropriate verse for you to take to God in prayer.

7. *Class teachers using this course for group study will find some helpful suggestions on page 63.*

how to
take the self-check tests

Each lesson is concluded with a test designed to help you evaluate what you have learned.

1. Review the lesson carefully in the light of the self-check test questions.

2. If there are any questions in the self-check test you cannot answer, perhaps you have written into your lesson the wrong answer from your Bible. Go over your work carefully to make sure you have filled in the blanks correctly.

3. When you think you are ready to take the self-check test, do so without looking up the answers.

4. Check your answers to the self-check test carefully with the answer key given on page 64.

5. If you have any questions wrong, your answer key will tell you where to find the correct answer in your lesson. Go back and locate the right answers. Learn by your mistakes!

apply
what you have learned
to your own life

In this connection, read carefully JAMES 1:22-25. It is only as you apply your lessons to your own life that you will really grow in grace and increase in the knowledge of God.

2

I John

By the period of A. D. 85-90 the Church was faced with internal heresy. False teachers were entering into the group proclaiming heresies. There was also a lack of brotherly love on the part of some of the brethren, particularly those who had more material gain than others. For these major reasons and other minor ones, John writes to his "little children."

The text itself lends no indication as to whom the letter was written. It was apparently directed to a group of churches rather than a single church. Some suggest that it was the group of churches surrounding Ephesus.

That John places such a heavy emphasis on the deity of Christ and his relationship to the Father is not surprising. The Gnostics of that day believed that matter was evil. They attacked the person of Christ. They attempted to make Christ less than the divine Son of God who was an equal member of the Trinity. The Gnostics maintained that Christ came upon the man Jesus at His baptism and left Him at the cross.

The epistle is rich with practical truths for the modern-day Christian. John offers a guideline for godly living in the midst of internal and external trouble in the church.

John's first epistle is a source of problems to many who think he teaches that salvation might be lost if the believer sins. This is due to a weak rendering of the English text. John actually teaches that the person who continually sins as a way of life is not a believer, because he never did yield to Christ. The constant sin in his life is proof that he never belonged to Christ.

Outline

Relationship of Christ to the Believer and the Believer to His Brother

I JOHN 1:1—2:14

John introduces the first of his three epistles with a discussion of fellowship and the problem of sin in the life. He presents the Christian's answer to sin.

Testimony regarding the incarnation

1. Name three ways in which John had contact with the Word of Life.

1:1 _____

_____

_____

2. What proof does John offer the believer that Christ was manifested?

1:2 _____

_____

3. State one of John's purposes for telling about Christ.

1:3 _____

_____

4. Name two of the members of the Trinity having fellowship with believers.

1:3 _____

_____

5. State one reason that John is writing this epistle.

1:4 _____

_____

_____

The sin question

6. What message is John passing on to his readers?

1:5 _____

_____

7. What makes liars out of us?

1:6 _____

8. State the basis of fellowship between two believers.

1:7 _____

_____

9. How are we cleansed of sin?

1:7 _____

_____

10. How is it possible for us to deceive ourselves?

1:8 _____

_____

The Gnostics held the view that matter was evil but the soul was not contaminated by the body. For this reason they said they had no sin. But John states that all have sinned and the sin remains until the blood of Christ removes it.

11. What must we do to have our sins forgiven?

1:9 ——————————————————————————

————————————————————————————————

12. How often will Christ forgive us our sins?

1:9 ——————————————————————————

————————————————————————————————

13. When we confess our sins, what else does Christ do besides forgiving us?

1:9 ——————————————————————————

14. What two conditions exist if we try to say that we have not sinned?

1:10 —————————————————————————

————————————————————————————————

————————————————————————————————

15. What is another of John's purposes for writing 1:1-10?

2:1 ——————————————————————————

————————————————————————————————

16. If a person does sin, what help is available to him?

2:1 ——————————————————————————

————————————————————————————————

An advocate is one called to the aid of another. It is a judicial term, meaning a pleader. In the Scriptures the word is used only in John's writings (see 14:16, 26; 15:26; 16:7 of his Gospel where it is translated "Comforter"). The Holy Spirit is presently God's Advocate to men on earth while Christ is man's Advocate in heaven. The same idea is also found in ROMANS 8:26-39 and HEBREWS 7:25.

7

17. For whose sins did Christ make propitiation?

2:2 _____

_____

The word "propitiate" refers to God's grace in sending Christ to die for our sins. By doing so, Christ met the Father's legal demands of death for those who are sinners.

18. How may we tell whether or not we know Christ?

2:3 _____

_____

19. What are we if we claim to keep Christ's commands when we actually do not?

2:4 _____

20. In what relation do we stand to the truth if we lie?

2:4 _____

_____

21. How may we have the love of God perfected in us?

2:5 _____

_____

22. Of what is this perfection a test?

2:5 _____

_____

23. What ultimately happens to those who claim to keep Christ's commandments but do not bear fruit?

JOHN 15:2 _____

_____

24. If a person claims to abide in Christ, what should he do?

2:6 _____

_____

John does not use "walk" in the literal sense of moving oneself forward by use of the legs and feet. He is referring to the believer's daily spiritual life. William's translates "walk" in Colossians 1:10 as "leading a life." It has to do with the outward life as seen by men.

25. What is the purpose of abiding in Christ?

John 15:4 _____

_____

26. What promise is made to those who abide?

John 15:7 _____

_____

A. T. Robertson says that "this astounding command and promise . . . is not without conditions and limitations. It involves such intimate union and harmony with Christ that nothing will be asked out of accord with the mind of Christ and so of the Father. Christ's name is mentioned in 15:16."

27. What is our standard for walking as Christians in our daily life?

2:6 _____

_____

_____

The new commandment

28. How may we test whether the new commandment is true or not?

2:8 _____

_____

29. By what means may we know that we are in the light?

2:9 _____

_____

30. Contrast the difference between the one who hates his brother and the one who loves his brother.

2:9, 10 _____

_____

_____

_____

31. What do we avoid if we abide in the light?

2:10 _____

The word "stumbling" is rendered "offense" in the Greek language. It may be anything which causes a brother to sin. See ROMANS 14:15.

32. Tell three things about the person who hates his brother.

2:11 _____

_____

_____

33. What is the cause of the preceding condition?

2:11 _____

_____

Separation from the world

34. Why is John writing this epistle to the little children?
2:12; cf. 2:1 _____

_____

_____

35. Give the reason for John's writing to the fathers.
2:13 _____

_____

In distinguishing the three groups to which John is writing, Robert S. Chandlish says, "As such, as little children, he first addresses them all, and appeals to them all collectively. But then, secondly, he separates them into two classes—'fathers' and 'young men'—old and spiritually exercised Christians on the one hand, and those who are in the fresh and vigorous prime of recent but yet manly Christian experience. All alike are 'little children'; but some are 'fathers,' ripe for glory; others are 'young men,' strong for work."

36. Why does John write to the young men?
2:13 _____

_____

37. What does John add to his message to the young men in 2:14 that he did not include in 2:13?

_____

_____

check-up time No. 1

You have just studied some important truths about present-day problems related to the question of sin in the believer's life and the believer's love for the brethren. Review your study by rereading the questions and your written answers. If you are not sure of an answer, reread the Scripture portion given to find the answer. Then take the test to see how well you understand the important truths you have studied.

In the right-hand margin write "True" or "False" after each of the following statements.

1. We are cleansed from sin through Christ's life. ⎯⎯⎯⎯⎯⎯

2. If we confess our sins to Christ, we will be forgiven. ⎯⎯⎯⎯⎯⎯

3. When we are forgiven by Christ, He also cleanses us from all unrighteousness. ⎯⎯⎯⎯⎯⎯

4. We can be sure that we love Christ if we attend church faithfully. ⎯⎯⎯⎯⎯⎯

5. We are called hypocrites if we say that we keep Christ's commandments when we do not. ⎯⎯⎯⎯⎯⎯

6. Even if we are liars, the truth still remains in us. ⎯⎯⎯⎯⎯⎯

7. We are abiding in Christ when we walk as He walked. ⎯⎯⎯⎯⎯⎯

8. We are not walking in the light if we hate one of the brethren. ⎯⎯⎯⎯⎯⎯

9. John wrote to the "little children" because their sins were forgiven. ⎯⎯⎯⎯⎯⎯

10. The "young men" referred to in John's first epistle had overcome Satan. ⎯⎯⎯⎯⎯⎯

Turn to page 64 and check your answers.

Warnings About the World and Heretical Teaching

I JOHN 2:15-29

Love of the world

Having established the reality of the incarnation and spoken on the subjects of sin, love of the brethren, and separation from darkness, John now deals with the worldly, heretical teaching that has entered in through the sect known as Gnostics.

1. John commands the Christian to refrain from loving two things. What are they?

2:15 _____

_____

2. How may a person judge whether or not the love of the Father is in him?

2:15 _____

_____

3. What three categories describe the sins of the world?

2:16 _____

_____

_____

The word for "world" in 2:16 does not refer to the physical world in which we live. Rather, it is used figuratively to denote human life and society devoid of God.

4. What two things will pass away?

2:17 _____

5. What will happen to the world?

HEBREWS 1:10, 11 _____

_____

This is a reference to the world or earth which we walk upon. A contrast is made between this world and that of I JOHN 2:16.

6. In what way is the Lord's eternality compared with the age of the world?

HEBREWS 1:11a, 12b _____

_____

7. When the world and its sin have passed away, what will happen to the person who does God's will?

2:17 _____

_____

Antichrist and antichrists

8. What proof does John give that it is the last time?

2:18 _____

_____

There is only one antichrist. He is mentioned in DANIEL 9:26, 27. But there were many abroad in John's day who had the spirit of antichrist. These were found in the ranks of the Gnostics. They had been a part of the visible church yet denied Christ. There are many today who also have this spirit.

9. How are those having the spirit of antichrist recognized?

2:19 _____

_____

10. How may a believer and one who has the spirit of antichrist be contrasted?

2:20 _____

_____

"Unction" or "anointing" primarily means anointing oil, but in this context it refers to the salvation which we receive from Christ (cf. II CORINTHIANS 1:21, 22). "Ye know all things" refers to the believer's understanding of the facts relating to Christ.

11. Having made the distinction between the believer and those who have the spirit of antichrist, what further reason does John give for writing?

2:21 _____

_____

12. How will the antichrist be recognizable?

2:22 _____

_____

13. What is the characteristic of those who deny the Son?

2:23 _____

14. After contrasting the antichrists and the believer, what does John tell the believer to do?

2:24 _____

_____

15. What has the believer heard from the beginning?

1:1, 5 _____

_____

15

16. Who paid the price for our sins?

2:2 _____

_____

17. How may we know that "that which ye have heard from the beginning" will remain?

II Timothy 1:12b _____

_____

18. What are the conditions for continuing in the Son?

2:24 _____

_____

19. How do we maintain a continuing fellowship with the Son?

1:7 _____

_____

20. What must be kept besides the walk if we are to sustain fellowship?

2:5 _____

_____

21. Why does continuing in the Son provide for continuation in the Father?

John 14:6, 9, 10 _____

_____

22. What has Christ promised to those who abide?

2:25 _____

_____

23. Name two other benefits of remaining in Christ.

JOHN 15:11; cf. I JOHN 1:4 —————————————————

—————————————————————————————————————

—————————————————————————————————————

"Remain" here refers to a fruitful relationship to Christ rather than to the possibility of loss of salvation. This is not taught by John in any of his writings.

24. What preparations are now being made for us in eternity?

JOHN 14: 2, 3 ————————————————————————

—————————————————————————————————————

—————————————————————————————————————

25. With whom will we dwell in eternity?

REVELATION 21:3 ——————————————————————

26. Name three of the conditions that will prevail during eternity for the believer.

REVELATION 21:4 ——————————————————————

—————————————————————————————————————

27. According to John, how is eternal life obtained?

JOHN 3:16 ——————————————————————————

—————————————————————————————————————

—————————————————————————————————————

28. What are the *these things* referred to in 2:26?

2:18, 22, 23 ————————————————————————

—————————————————————————————————————

29. Who are the ones seducing believers?

2:18 ————————————————————————————————

30. With what are these seducers linked?

I Timothy 4:1 ⎯⎯⎯⎯⎯⎯⎯⎯⎯⎯⎯⎯⎯⎯⎯⎯

⎯⎯⎯⎯⎯⎯⎯⎯⎯⎯⎯⎯⎯⎯⎯⎯⎯⎯⎯⎯⎯⎯⎯⎯

The believer's possessions and hope

31. What safeguard do we have against seducers of our faith?

2:27 ⎯⎯⎯⎯⎯⎯⎯⎯⎯⎯⎯⎯⎯⎯⎯⎯⎯⎯⎯⎯

⎯⎯⎯⎯⎯⎯⎯⎯⎯⎯⎯⎯⎯⎯⎯⎯⎯⎯⎯⎯⎯⎯⎯⎯

32. Why is there no need for any man to teach a believer?

2:27 ⎯⎯⎯⎯⎯⎯⎯⎯⎯⎯⎯⎯⎯⎯⎯⎯⎯⎯⎯⎯

⎯⎯⎯⎯⎯⎯⎯⎯⎯⎯⎯⎯⎯⎯⎯⎯⎯⎯⎯⎯⎯⎯⎯⎯

"That any man teach you" is better rendered "that anyone keep on teaching you." With Christ dwelling within and the Holy Spirit teaching them all things, they did not need anyone to re-tell them of what they had in Christ compared to the false teaching of the Gnostics.

33. In what way are we to use that which we know?

Matthew 28:19, 20 ⎯⎯⎯⎯⎯⎯⎯⎯⎯⎯⎯⎯⎯⎯

⎯⎯⎯⎯⎯⎯⎯⎯⎯⎯⎯⎯⎯⎯⎯⎯⎯⎯⎯⎯⎯⎯⎯⎯

34. What reason for abiding in Christ does John give?

2:28 ⎯⎯⎯⎯⎯⎯⎯⎯⎯⎯⎯⎯⎯⎯⎯⎯⎯⎯⎯⎯

⎯⎯⎯⎯⎯⎯⎯⎯⎯⎯⎯⎯⎯⎯⎯⎯⎯⎯⎯⎯⎯⎯⎯⎯

35. What will happen before Christ appears?

II Thessalonians 2:1-5 ⎯⎯⎯⎯⎯⎯⎯⎯⎯⎯⎯

⎯⎯⎯⎯⎯⎯⎯⎯⎯⎯⎯⎯⎯⎯⎯⎯⎯⎯⎯⎯⎯⎯⎯⎯

36. Describe the appearing of the Lord.

I CORINTHIANS 15:52 _____

_____

37. What additional information is added in I THESSALONIANS 4: 16, 17?

_____

_____

_____

38. Because Christ is returning for us, what should our attitude be?

I CORINTHIANS 15:58 _____

_____

_____

check-up time No. 2

You have just studied some important truths about present-day problems relating to the world and false teachers. Review your study by rereading the questions and your written answers. If you aren't sure of an answer, reread the Scripture portion given to see if you can find the answer. Then take this test to see how well you understand important truths you have studied.

In the right-hand margin write "True" or "False" after each of the following statements.

1. The Christian may love the material things of this world but not love the world.   _____

2. The sin of worldliness may be categorized into five major categories.   _____

3. The antichrist will deny the Father and the Son.   _____

4. Our sins are paid for by Christ.   _____

5. The saved will dwell with God in eternity.   _____

6. There are many antichrists seducing believers.   _____

7. Christ dwelling in us is a safeguard against false teachers.   _____

8. Every believer will be confident at the appearing of Christ.   _____

9. The day of Christ will come before the man of sin is revealed.   _____

10. We should remain steadfast because Christ is returning for us.   _____

Turn to page 64 and check your answers.

A Consistent Life and the Proofs of Salvation

I JOHN 3:1-24

Exhortations regarding a consistent life

Having revealed the Gnostics as antichrists, John develops the theme of the life of the believer, which he began in the second chapter.

1. What has the Father given us?

3:1 _____

_____

2. Because of the love bestowed upon us by the Father, what is our inherited position?

3:1 _____

_____

3. If we are children of God, what are we in relation to Christ?

ROMANS 8:16, 17 _____

_____

_____

4. Why are we not known by the world?

3:1 _____

_____

5. At what point in time will the sons of God be fully like Christ?

3:2 _____

6. To what extent will we see Christ upon His return?

3:2 _____

_____

7. Every Christian who is waiting for Christ's return has a particular type of life to lead. What is it?

3:3 _____

_____

8. Who is a pattern for purity in the life of the Christian?

3:3 _____

9. Give a definition of sin.

3:4 _____

10. Why did Christ come down to earth?

3:5; cf. JOHN 3:17 _____

_____

_____

11. How may we avoid sin?

3:6 _____

_____

This is a reference to the person who does not habitually sin.

12. What is the legal position of the person who accepts Christ?

3:7 _____

_____

13. What type of person is of the devil?

3:8 _____

_____

"Committeth" is "doing" in the Greek text. It has the idea of one who is continually sinning rather than the one who commits one sin.

14. Why was Christ born on the earth?

3:8 _____

_____

15. Why does the Christian refrain from continually sinning as a pattern of life?

3:9 _____

_____

16. By not leading a life given over to sin with whom are the children of God in contrast?

3:10 _____

_____

17. What two actions characterize the one who lives in sin?

3:10 _____

_____

_____

18. In contrast to the one living in sin, what should the Christian do?

3:11 _____

_____

19. Describe the example given to illustrate the truth of 3:11.

3:12; cf. GENESIS 4:8 _____

_____

Tests of salvation

20. What is the strong comparison used of the one who hates his brother?

3:15 _____

_____

21. Since Christ gave his life for us, what should we do for our brethren, if necessary?

3:16 _____

_____

22. If a Christian has wealth, how is he to use it?

3:17 _____

_____

23. Under what condition does wealth and its use constitute a sin?

3:17 _____

_____

_____

24. What is the spiritual condition of the Christian who has ignored a brother's need?

3:17 _____

25. State two inadequate ways of trying to show Christian love.

3:18 _____

26. State two positive ways of demonstrating Christian love.

3:18 _____

27. How may we know that we are living in truth?

3:18, 19 _____

_____

28. If we love in deed and truth and yet our heart condemns us, what may we rely on?

3:20 _____

_____

_____

29. How great a knowledge does God have of the heart of man?

3:20 _____

_____

30. What gives us confidence toward God?

3:21 _____

_____

31. How much will we receive of what we ask for?

3:22 _____

32. What must we do to be assured of receiving what we ask for?

3:22 _____

_____

_____

_____

33. What is God's commandment to Christians regarding Christ?

3:23 _____

_____

34. What is God's commandment regarding our relationship with one another?

3:23 _____

_____

_____

35. What must we do in order for Christ to dwell in us?

3:24 _____

_____

36. How may we know that Christ dwells in us?

3:24 _____

_____

_____

check-up time No. 3

You have just studied some important truths about the Christian's consistent life and how he may know that he is saved. Review your study by rereading the questions and your written answers. If you aren't sure of an answer, reread the Scripture portion given to see if you can find the answer. Then take this test to see how well you understand important truths you have studied.

In the right-hand margin write "True" or "False" after each of the following statements.

1. Every believer has the love of the Father. _____

2. The world does not know Christ or His children. _____

3. When Christ comes, we will see Him as He is. _____

4. The Christian may set his own goals for purity. _____

5. Christ's purpose for coming to earth was to take away our sin. _____

6. Christ came to save sinners rather than to defeat the works of the devil. _____

7. Righteousness is one contrast between the children of God and the children of the devil. _____

8. To hate your brother is a serious offense. _____

9. A Christian sins if he keeps a bank account. _____

10. The believer must show his love in a practical way. _____

Turn to page 64 and check your answers.

False Teachers and the Christian's Life of Love

I JOHN 4:1-21

The spirit of truth and the spirit of error

Once again John returns to a discussion of the false teachers. He gives additional marks which identify the false teacher in contrast to the child of God. Knowing the division which is brought in on the coat tail of false teaching, John also exhorts the brethren to love one another.

1. What is every believer to do when he sits under the ministry of a teacher or preacher?

4:1 _____

_____

2. Why is it necessary to try the spirits?

4:1 _____

_____

3. What test may be used to try the teachers?

4:2 _____

_____

4. What distinction is made between the Spirit of God and the spirits?

4:2 _____

_____

_____

5. What relationship to God, if any, does a teacher or preacher have if he denies that Jesus came in the flesh?

4:3 _____

6. What spirit does this denial represent?

4:3 _____

_____

7. When will the spirit of antichrist be present in the world?

4:3 _____

_____

8. What contrast is made between the "little children" and the spirit of antichrist?

4:4 _____

_____

_____

9. Why have the children of God overcome the false teachers?

4:4 _____

_____

10. Where does the false teacher place his affections?

4:5 _____

_____

11. How does the world react to the false teacher in contrast to the child of God?

4:5; cf. 3:1 _____

_____

12. How does the believer respond to the one who knows God?

4:6 _____

_____

13. How may the spirit of truth and the spirit of error be determined?

4:6 _____

_____

Brotherly love

14. What is the source of Christian love for the brethren?

4:7 _____

15. What two things does John say about the believer who loves the brethren?

4:7 _____

_____

_____

16. Why can a believer who does not love the brethren, not know God?

4:8 _____

_____

17. How was the love of God manifested toward us?

4:9 _____

_____

18. How does John describe Christ?

4:9 _____

The Greek text makes "only begotten" more emphatic with the rendering *His Son, the only begotten.*

19. Why was Christ sent?

4:9 _____

_____

20. What clarification does John add regarding the love of God?

4:10 _____

_____

21. What is Christ's relationship to our sins?

4:10; cf. 2:2 _____

_____

22. What basis does the believer have for loving other Christians?

4:11 _____

_____

23. How many men have seen God?

4:12; cf. JOHN 1:18 _____

_____

24. How may we know that God dwells in us?

4:12 _____

_____

25. What happens to the love of Christ which dwells in us?

4:12 _____

26. How may we know that we dwell in Christ?

4:13 _____

_____

27. What is John's personal testimony regarding Christ?

4:14 _____

Christ's death made provision for everyone to be saved (JOHN 1:12), but only those who accept Him will be saved (ROMANS 10:13).

28. For how many people of the world is Christ the Saviour?

4:14; cf. JOHN 1:12 _____

_____

29. In whom does God dwell?

4:15 _____

_____

30. What testimony does John personally give regarding the love of God?

4:16 _____

_____

31. What is the relationship between the one who dwells in love and God?

4:16 _____

_____

32. What is our position at the day of judgment because of our love for God?

4:17 _____

_____

33. What removes fear?

4:18 _____

34. What results in the life of the person who fears?

4:18 _____

35. Why do we love God?

4:19 _____

_____

36. How does this compare with God's love for us?

4:10 _____

_____

37. In what way may the believer prove his love for God whom he has never seen?

4:20 _____

_____

_____

38. What is God's commandment to the Christian?

4:21 _____

check-up time No. 4

You have just studied some important truths about false teachers and the Christian's life of love. Review your study by rereading the questions and your written answers. If you aren't sure of an answer, reread the Scripture portion given to see if you can find the answer. Then take this test to see how well you understand important truths you have studied.

In the right-hand margin write "True" or "False" after each of the following statements.

1. The Christian should never question the teaching of a pastor or teacher. _____

2. False teachers may be detected because they deny that Christ came in the flesh. _____

3. The spirit of antichrist ceased to exist after the day of Pentecost. _____

4. The spirit of antichrist is too powerful for Christians to resist. _____

5. God's love is manifested to us through Christ. _____

6. According to John, no man has seen God. _____

7. We may know that God dwells in us if we love the brethren. _____

8. Christ died for the sins of the whole world. _____

9. It is possible for the believer to have boldness at the day of judgment. _____

10. We love God because He first loved us. _____

Turn to page 64 and check your answers.

Faith, Assurance and the Believer's Understanding

I John 5:1-21

The outworking of faith

John concludes his epistle by presenting faith as the all-pervading principle which will see the believer through conflict.

1. Who is born of God?

5:1 _____

_____

2. How may we tell that we love other believers?

5:2 _____

_____

3. How is the love of God displayed in the life of the believer?

5:3 _____

_____

4. Who has the power to overcome the world?

5:4 _____

_____

5. What is used in the life of the believer to overcome the world?

5:4 _____

_____

6. Who can overcome the world?

5:5 _____

7. How did Christ come, according to John?

5:6 _____

_____

A great deal of controversy arises over the meaning of "water and blood." One possible answer is that it refers to His baptism and His death on the cross.

8. Who bears witness to Christ's coming, and why?

5:6 _____

_____

9. Name the three persons who bear witness in heaven.

5:7 _____

_____

The thought of Christ as the "Word" is further developed by John in JOHN 1:1-3, 14. The Gnostics would not place Christ in a position of equality with The Father and the Spirit, but John is very careful to make this point clear.

10. Name the three that bear witness on earth.

5:8 _____

_____

11. Whose witness is the greatest according to John?

5:9 _____

_____

John's argument runs that if we accept the witness of man, which we do, certainly God's witness is greater than man's, and God has testified concerning His Son. Therefore, we should accept His Son.

12. Who has the witness within himself?

5:10 _____

_____

13. Why is it a serious matter to disbelieve God's Word?

5:10 _____

_____

14. When a person challenges God's Word, what does that person become?

Romans 3:4 _____

_____

15. What has God given to the believer?

5:11 _____

_____

16. In whom does this life dwell, and upon whom does it depend?

5:11 _____

17. What is the difference between the believer and the non-believer?

5:12 _____

_____

Assurance and its outworking

18. What additional purpose does John now give as a reason for writing?

5:13a ————————————————————————————————

19. What is John's further reason for writing?

5:13b ————————————————————————————————

——————————————————————————————————————

20. What must we do if God is to hear our petition?

5:14 —————————————————————————————————

——————————————————————————————————————

21. Of what are we assured if He hears us?

5:15 —————————————————————————————————

——————————————————————————————————————

To study the various conditions necessary if prayer is to be answered, see the course *How to Pray*, which is another study in this *Teach Yourself the Bible Series*.

22. If we see a brother sinning, what are we to do?

5:16 —————————————————————————————————

——————————————————————————————————————

23. If we pray, what will happen to the brother?

5:16 —————————————————————————————————

——————————————————————————————————————

24. How should we pray regarding the sin unto death?

5:16 —————————————————————————————————

——————————————————————————————————————

Such references as I Corinthians 3:17; 5:1-5; 11:30 support the teaching that it is possible for a believer to go so far in sin as to call for unusual disciplinary action on the part of God. A believer thus judged does not lose his salvation, although his human life is shortened.

25. What constitutes sin?

5:17 _____

_____

Facts known to the believer

26. What does the believer do regarding sin?

5:18 _____

_____

27. In what way may Satan affect the believer?

5:18 _____

_____

28. What is the condition of the believer in contrast to the condition of the world?

5:19 _____

_____

29. What has Christ given to the believer?

5:20 _____

_____

30. Why does Christ give us this understanding?

5:20 _____

_____

31. What are we to do as "little children"?

5:21 _____

_____

Idols are often images or objects set aside for religious worship. John is not referring just to this type of idol. Believers who do not worship images often worship such things as money, success, etc. An idol may be anything which is given preeminence before God or comes between God and the believer.

check-up time No. 5

You have just studied some important truths about faith and assurance. Review your study by rereading the questions and your written answers. If you aren't sure of an answer, reread the Scripture portion given to see if you can find the answer. Then take this test to see how well you understand important truths you have studied.

In the right-hand margin write "True" or "False" after each of the following statements.

1. Both Christians and non-Christians have the power to overcome the world. _____

2. According to John, prayer is the victory that overcomes the world. _____

3. The Father, Son, and Holy Spirit bear witness to Christ in heaven. _____

4. God's witness is greater than man's. _____

5. The person who does not believe God infers that God is a liar. _____

6. A believer may be distinguished from the unbeliever because the believer has Christ. _____

7. If we ask for things according to God's will, He will answer our requests. _____

8. A true believer keeps himself from sin. _____

9. According to John, the whole world is wicked. _____

10. John concludes his first epistle by telling us to refrain from every appearance of evil. _____

Turn to page 64 and check your answers.

II John

Modern scholars usually agree that all three epistles of John were written by the same man, but they all seem to have differences of opinion as to whom John was writing in II JOHN. Some say it is a church, while others take the word "lady" to refer to one of the leading women of a local church. Though scholars cannot settle the question of who is the recipient of John's second epistle, its value is unaffected.

The epistle, written about the same time as I JOHN, deals with the similar theme of false teachers and love for the brethren.

Outline

1. Appreciation to the Elect Lady 1-4

2. Instruction on the Believer's Walk 5-6

3. Warnings Against Deceivers 7-11

Christian Love, Truth, and a Test for False Teachers

II JOHN 1-13

Appreciation to the elect lady

In his second epistle, John is once again dealing with Christian love. He is relating it to truth, which is a key word in this epistle.

1. In what way does John love the elect lady?

1 _____

2. Where does the truth dwell, according to John?

2 _____

3. How long will the truth dwell in the believer?

2 _____

4. What is the source of mercy and peace?

3 _____

5. How is the grace from the Father and the Son given to us?

3 _____

6. What did John find regarding the walk of the children?

4 _____

_____

7. Why did this please John?

4b _____

_____

Instruction on the believer's walk

8. On what basis does John beseech the lady?

5 _____

_____

9. What is the commandment given by John?

5 _____

_____

10. What is love as defined by John?

6 _____

_____

11. What is the believer to do in relation to the commandment?

6 _____

_____

Warnings against deceivers

12. By what may a deceiver be known?

7 _____

_____

13. What is John's exhortation regarding the labors of the workers?

8 _____

_____

14. Why should we hold on to what we have gained spiritually?

8b _____

_____

15. What description is given of the person who transgresses?

9 _____

16. What does a person have who abides in the doctrine of Christ?

9 _____

17. How are we to treat a person who does not believe in the doctrine of Christ?

10 _____

_____

18. Why should we refuse to bid a false teacher God speed?

11 _____

_____

19. Why does John hope to see the lady personally?

12 _____

_____

check-up time No. 6

You have just studied some important truths about Christian love, truth, and a test for false teachers. Review your study by rereading the questions and your written answers. If you aren't sure of an answer, reread the Scripture portion given to see if you can find the answer. Then take this test to see how well you understand important truths you have studied.

In the right-hand margin write "True" or "False" after each of the following statements.

1. John opens his second epistle by saying that he loves the elect lady in goodness. _____

2. Truth will remain with the believer forever. _____

3. According to John, mercy and peace come from the Father and the Son. _____

4. John rejoiced that the elect lady's children walked in grace. _____

5. "Tell others about Christ" is the commandment to which John refers as being from the beginning. _____

6. We show love if we walk after his commandments. _____

7. A deceiver is one who misinterprets the teaching regarding love of the brethren. _____

8. The person committing transgression abides in God. _____

9. The person abiding in the doctrine of Christ has both the Father and the Son. _____

10. We should extend every Christian hospitality to misguided false teachers. _____

Turn to page 64 and check your answers.

III John

This epistle, the shortest book in the New Testament, was penned by John about the same time he wrote his other two. Though the epistle is directed to Gaius, there are several men by that name mentioned in Scripture to whom it could have been addressed. Paul was accompanied on his third missionary journey by Gaius of Macedonia (ACTS 19:29). There was also a Gaius who lived in Derbe (ACTS 20:4), as well as one in Corinth (I CORINTHIANS 1:14).

John wrote to Gaius because of trouble directed against the apostle by Diotrephes who was attempting to exalt himself above the others in the church. This book is particularly pertinent to the present-day church and the problems which it faces.

Outline

1. A Commendation to Gaius 1-8

2. A Rebuke to Diotrephes 9-10

3. Demetrius and John's Future Visit 11-14

Ministering Brethren, a Good and Bad Example

III JOHN 1-14

A commendation to Gaius

The third epistle written by John has more of an emphasis upon the saints who are rightly related to Christ and the church. Diotrephes, however, is an example of the opposite. He well represents many present-day church members who seek prominence in the church.

1. In what way is John's love for Gaius and his love for the elect lady of II JOHN alike?

1; cf. II JOHN 2 _____

_____

_____

2. What is John's desire for the physical well-being of his readers?

2 _____

_____

3. How is their physical well-being compared to their spiritual prosperity?

2 _____

_____

4. What report should be received of all Christians?

3 _____

_____

5. How should the Christian walk in his daily life?

3 _____

_____

6. What should our ultimate joy be regarding those who have been influenced by our ministry?

4 _____

7. What type of service should we give to both brethren and strangers?

5 _____

_____

8. If we serve others well, what blessing is in store?

6 _____

_____

9. In what service may we do well?

6 _____

_____

10. For what reason does the Lord's servant witness?

7 _____

11. What should be our attitude regarding remuneration for our spiritual services from the unsaved?

7 _____

_____

12. According to II JOHN 10, we are not to receive false teachers. Who should we receive?

8 _____

13. What blessing will we receive if we extend our fellowship and hospitality to faithful Christian workers?

8 _____

_____

A rebuke to Diotrephes

14. Why was John's writing not accepted in the church of which Diotrephes was a member?

9 _____

_____

15. What is John's attitude toward Diotrephes?

10 _____

_____

16. What was Diotrephes' attitude toward his fellow Christians?

10 _____

_____

_____

17. What action did Diotrephes take against the believers?

10 _____

Demetrius and John's future visit

18. What path should the Christian always take?

11 _____

_____

19. How may the Christian tell who belongs to God and who does not?

11 _____

_____

20. What does Demetrius do in contrast to Diotrephes?

12 _____

_____

21. What are John's plans for the future?

13, 14 _____

_____

_____

_____

check-up time No. 7

You have just studied some important truths about brethren who are faithful in their ministry and how they should be received. Review your study by rereading the questions and your written answers. If you aren't sure of an answer, reread the Scripture portion given to see if you can find the answer. Then take this test to see how well you understand important truths you have studied.

In the right-hand margin write "True" or "False" after each of the following statements.

1. John loves all believers in truth. _____

2. John is interested in the physical as well as spiritual well-being of the believers. _____

3. The Christian should walk in truth. _____

4. We should offer faithful service to brethren and strangers alike. _____

5. If we do offer faithful service, we will do well. _____

6. We should receive false teachers but be cautious. _____

7. Diotrephes helped in promoting John's teaching. _____

8. John speaks out against Diotrephes in his third epistle. _____

9. Diotrephes had difficulty in getting along with the brethren. _____

10. Demetrius shared the same views as Diotrephes. _____

Turn to page 64 and check your answers.

Jude

JUDE was written by Judas, the brother of the Lord (v. 1; see MARK 6:3). Written about A. D. 75, this epistle was intended to expose the false teachers who had entered into the Church. Judas also writes to prepare the flock so that they will not be swayed by the false doctrine being taught.

The book is closely related to II PETER which also deals with the false teachers. Both books were describing the present conditions but also predicting what would become a greater struggle for the Church in the years beyond.

Little is known as to the exact destination of Jude's epistle. It is definitely Jewish in interest, leading some to suggest Palestine, Asia Minor, or Alexandria. Though the book is Jewish in nature, it should be addressed to all Christians.

Outline

1. Contending for the Faith 1-4

2. Revealing the False Teachers 5-13

3. Judging the Wicked 14-19

4. Encouraging the Believer 20-25

Instruction Regarding False Teachers

JUDE 1-25

Contending for the faith

Jude offers the believer a guideline for detecting false teachers and apostates. He uses historical examples to prove that association with apostasy brings God's judgment.

1. What is the source of our sanctification?

1 _____

_____

2. What two things does Christ do for the believer?

1 _____

_____

_____

3. What greeting does Jude use with those who are under the teaching of false teachers?

2 _____

_____

4. State Jude's original purpose for writing.

3 _____

_____

5. What purpose for writing superseded Jude's original intention?

3 _____

_____

6. What exhortation did Jude deliver to the brethren?

3 _____

_____

_____

The Greek word for "contend" is the same from which we derive our English word "agony." If believers do not work to preserve the faith, false doctrines will take over as a normal course of events.

7. How does the false teacher enter into the group?

4 _____

_____

The idea presented is that of a thief sneaking in through a side door.

8. What do the false teachers do with the grace of God?

4 _____

_____

"Lasciviousness" may be defined as license which sets aside the claims of Christ for the claims of sin.

9. What is the false teacher's doctrine concerning the person of Christ?

4; cf. I John 4:3 _____

_____

Revealing the false teachers

10. Of what historical incident does Jude remind his readers?

5; cf. Exodus 23:20, 33 —————————————————

————————————————————————————————

11. Why did God destroy a part of the Jewish nation after delivering them from Egypt?

5 ——————————————————————————————

————————————————————————————————

12. What other illustration of historical apostasy does Jude use?

6 ——————————————————————————————

————————————————————————————————

13. What is the present condition of the fallen angels?

6 ——————————————————————————————

————————————————————————————————

14. What is the third historical example of apostasy?

7; cf. Deuteronomy 29:23 ———————————————

————————————————————————————————

15. Why were Sodom and Gomorrah destroyed?

7; cf. Genesis 19:24 —————————————————

————————————————————————————————

————————————————————————————————

16. Of what is the destruction of the two cities an example?

7 ——————————————————————————————

————————————————————————————————

17. In comparing the instances of historical apostasy, what does Jude call the false teachers?

8 _____

_____

18. What do the false teachers do?

8 _____

_____

19. What example is used to teach us that we are not to speak evil of any man?

9 _____

_____

20. How are we to condemn false teachers?

9 _____

_____

21. Of what do the false teachers speak evil?

10 _____

_____

22. How does Jude describe the false teachers?

10 _____

_____

23. Name five ways in which Paul describes people such as the false teachers.

Romans 1:24-32 —————————————————————

—————————————————————————————

—————————————————————————————

—————————————————————————————

—————————————————————————————

24. In whose path have the false teachers followed?

11 ————————————————————————————

—————————————————————————————

25. What was Cain's sin?

Genesis 4:8 —————————————————————

—————————————————————————————

26. What is Jude's fifth example of historical apostasy?

11 ————————————————————————————

—————————————————————————————

27. What is the error of Balaam?

11; cf. Numbers 22-24 ————————————————————

—————————————————————————————

28. What sin did Core (Korah) commit?

Numbers 16 —————————————————————

—————————————————————————————

29. What occasion does the false teacher use to deceive the believers?

12 _____

_____

The love feast was a particularly sacred time preceding the communion service. It is comparable to false teachers using our communion service today to teach false doctrine.

30. How does Jude describe the false teachers?

12 _____

_____

Judging the wicked

31. What will God do to the false teachers?

14, 15 _____

32. Why are these people teaching false doctrine?

16b _____

_____

33. In the light of the false teachers, what is Jude's warning?

17, 18 _____

_____

Encouraging the believer

34. What are believers to do in the face of false doctrine?

20 _____

_____

35. How may believers gain spiritual strength to combat false doctrine?

20, 21 ————————————————————————————

————————————————————————————

————————————————————————————

36. Who keeps the true believer from falling into apostasy?

24 ————————————————————————————

37. What will our condition be when presented before the Father?

24 ————————————————————————————

————————————————————————————

check-up time No. 8

You have just studied some important truths about the apostasy of false teachers. Review your study by rereading the questions and your written answers. If you aren't sure of an answer, reread the Scripture portion given to see if you can find the answer. Then take this test to see how well you understand important truths you have studied.

In the right-hand margin write "True" or "False" after each of the following statements.

1. We are sanctified by God the Father. _____

2. Jude originally intended to write about the common salvation. _____

3. False teachers sometimes enter a group by professing to be prophets. _____

4. Jude uses the Israelites saved out of Egypt to illustrate judgment on apostates. _____

5. The people of Sodom and Gomorrah were destroyed because of wickedness. _____

6. Jude calls the false teachers filthy dreamers.

7. Even though false teachers are apostate, they do respect authority. _____

8. Jude says that it is permissible to revile false teachers. _____

9. Jude calls the false teachers brute beasts. _____

10. Believers are to build themselves up in faith and pray in the power of the Holy Spirit. _____

Turn to page 64 and check your answers.

Suggestions for class use

1. The class teacher may wish to tear this page from each workbook as the answer key is on the reverse side.

2. The teacher should study the lesson first, filling in the blanks in the workbook. He should be prepared to give help to the class on some of the harder places in the lesson. He should also take the self-check tests himself, check his answers with the answer key and look up any question answered incorrectly.

3. Class sessions can be supplemented by the teacher's giving a talk or leading a discussion on the subject to be studied. The class could then fill in the workbook together as a group, in teams, or individually. If so desired by the teacher, however, this could be done at home. The self-check tests can be done as homework by the class.

4. The self-check tests can be corrected at the beginning of each class session. A brief discussion of the answers can serve as review for the previous lesson.

5. The teacher should motivate and encourage his students. Some public recognition might well be given to class members who successfully complete this course.

answer key
to self-check tests

Be sure to look up any questions you answered incorrectly.

Q gives the number of the test *question*.

A gives the correct *answer*.

R *refers* you back to the place in the lesson itself where the correct answer is to be found.

Mark your wrong answers with an "x".

TEST 1			TEST 2			TEST 3			TEST 4		
Q	A	R	Q	A	R	Q	A	R	Q	A	R
1	F	9	1	F	1	1	T	1	1	F	1
2	T	11	2	F	3	2	T	4	2	T	4
3	T	13	3	T	12	3	T	6	3	F	7
4	F	18	4	T	16	4	F	8	4	F	9
5	F	19	5	T	25	5	T	10	5	T	17
6	F	20	6	T	29	6	F	14	6	T	23
7	T	24	7	T	31	7	T	16	7	T	24
8	T	29	8	F	34	8	T	20	8	T	28
9	T	34	9	F	35	9	F	23	9	T	32
10	T	36	10	T	38	10	T	26	10	T	35

TEST 5			TEST 6			TEST 7			TEST 8		
Q	A	R	Q	A	R	Q	A	R	Q	A	R
1	F	4	1	F	1	1	T	1	1	T	1
2	F	5	2	T	3	2	T	3	2	T	4
3	T	9	3	T	4	3	T	5	3	F	7
4	T	11	4	F	7	4	T	7	4	T	11
5	T	13	5	F	9	5	T	8	5	T	15
6	T	17	6	T	10	6	F	12	6	T	17
7	T	21	7	F	12	7	F	14	7	F	18
8	T	26	8	F	16	8	T	15	8	F	20
9	T	28	9	T	16	9	T	17	9	T	22
10	F	31	10	F	17	10	F	20	10	T	35

How well
did
you do?

0-1 wrong answers—excellent work

2-3 wrong answers—review errors carefully

4 or more wrong answers—restudy the lesson before going on to the next one